To Wilmer and Vivian
with many thanks from
Doug and Mims,
March 1988

Sydney

A Pictorial Contrast

SYDNEY
A Pictorial Contrast

Photography: Phil Gray

Concept: Peter McGill
Text: Nicholas Brash
Research: Christiane Brash

GOLDEN PRESS
SYDNEY · AUCKLAND

My Sydney

DAVID McNICOLL

SYDNEY'S MOST DISTINGUISHED
AND RESPECTED JOURNALIST. HE HAS
WRITTEN FOR THE BULLETIN AND THE
TELEGRAPHS SINCE BEFORE WORLD WAR II —
SEEING, ABSORBING AND LOVING THE CITY AND
THE HARBOUR

Sydneysiders, who tend to be completely enraptured with the city in which they live, have been known to say that anyone who doesn't live in Sydney is merely camping out. Is that going too far? Well, maybe a little . . . but only a little.

Sydney is a city blessed by nature and so far not destroyed by man, despite some pretty valiant efforts. It is beautifully formed, well placed, and it enjoys one of the best climates in the world. Reading history it is hard to understand some of the harsh things written about it by the early colonists. But then, life in Sydney's early days was not altogether pleasant — and it was little wonder that hardship produced unfavourable impressions.

In many ways, Sydney is probably more attractive today than it was in the hundred years after Phillip. The early watercolourists — the great Thomas Watling in the 1790's and Conrad Martens last century — show us a city of blue bays and sandy coves, with little habitation but lots of rather scrubby foliage. Today's enlivened Sydney with cheeky ferries and graceful yachts, with marinas and wharves, with great overseas vessels, with spires and highrise buildings — to me these things have given the city its vitality, and instead of detracting from its beauty, have added to the overall charm.

The arrival of the camera with its unforgiving eye was the start of clinical dissection of cities. No more could the romantic artist delete the ugly with carefully arranged colours. The camera told the story, warts and all, and the black and white result on the old photographic plates was devastatingly candid and accurate. This accuracy and eye for a subject was never better exemplified than in the remarkable

photographs from the EB Studios which form the 'early' part of the contrasting Sydney we examine in this book.

I first came to work in Sydney in 1933. It seems so long ago now. Young people look at me curiously when I talk about catching the last night tram up King Street on my way home to Rose Bay. They scratch their heads at the thought of taking a ferry to Manly, then a tram to Narrabeen and, if very lucky, an ancient taxi to go through to Palm Beach. As for the Bridge — they can scarcely believe there really was a vehicular ferry across the Harbour, and you had to take it if you wanted your car to get to the North Shore.

The EB photographs go back to 1917. Strangely, what was called 'the Great Australian Ugliness' was not as evident in the early suburban days as it became in the 30's and 40's as sprawl and overhead wire and pole masses took charge of outer areas.

Development round the Harbour itself has never gravely offended taste. In fact, development has brought improvements. The old whaling station in Mosman Bay went, and so did many of the ramshackle wharves and boatsheds. The Opera House, to the amazement of many early critics, became a thing of beauty and never-ending interest, a world wonder. The Bridge, although Sydney has had fifty years to get used to it, has never lost its charm, and the simplicity of its lines is a joy to the eye. The great highrise buildings of the city centre are best seen from the Harbour, and preferably by dawn or dusk.

It is easy to dwell too long on Sydney, the great maritime city. But there are other facets. Sydney to the West — the only way it can expand easily — has seen the creation of many tedious and unattractive suburbs. The 'sprawl', as it is known, was inevitable in a big city whose population was positively roaring up week by week. But in recent years the trend towards building unattractive boxes has eased, and the new homes in the outer suburbs are brick and neat.

From Manly, up the Peninsula, progress has seen new houses built with remarkable ingenuity on hills and above cliffs, facing the sea or the inland waterway of Pittwater. In the leafy fastnesses of the North Shore the homes of the comfortable professionals nestle in large grounds, surrounded by tennis courts, pools and prize gardens.

The homes of the Eastern Suburbs are probably the cream on the cake. Harbourside sites today bring prices in the millions, and not an eyebrow is raised. The view is the main consideration; or is it the chance of owning a jetty for one's yacht? Even away from the actual foreshores — provided the houses have a view of the harbour — the asking price runs into hundreds of thousands. What would Conrad Martens think today if he sat with his easel and brushes on Point Piper looking towards Vaucluse where, in his day, no house would

be found except the mansion of William Charles Wentworth and perhaps a few shacks round the shores.

This remarkable book of 'old and new' photographs goes into a detail which is quite extraordinary, and fills one with admiration not only for the skills but the tenacity of John Ennemark and Hilda Bridges. They captured a great deal of Sydney, and their work will give joy to many people who like to look back on older days and older ways.

Am I correct in my obsessive admiration for my city? Let me confess here and now, my feelings are not motivated merely by its beauty. It is the accessibility of sport and pleasure which makes Sydney almost unique in the world. Where does one find a city where the races are only minutes away, where the surf is a short bus trip from the city centre, where golf courses abound within the near suburban limits and where the joys of sailing are on the doorstep?

The eighties are very different from the twenties; they may not be so gracious, and they may indeed be raucous. But the years have not destroyed the charm and beauty of Sydney; they have merely fortified its paramount position as a city of majestic splendour.

My Sydney
BRIDGET ADAMS

BRIDGET ADAMS, 18. A GOLD COAST MODEL WITH
THE URSULA HUFNAGEL AGENCY WHO
'EMIGRATED' TO SYDNEY AT THE START OF 1985

Sydney's fantastic. Life just pumps out of it; every day you're here it's happening. I found it hard at first. I was lonely — I'd left home for the first time and here I was in this vast city. But now I find everywhere else is boring. There's more prospects in Sydney; more culture; more everything!

And I try to do everything. I go horse-riding in the outer west, the Rugby Union in winter and the beach in summer. I love all water sports and Sydney's just great with its beaches and the harbour. I love picnics and every week I find a new place. I think the big thing about Sydney is going out and being out. Maybe there's bad things but I just don't see them... I'm so busy seeing the good things!

SYDNEY — A PICTORIAL CONTRAST
was created and produced by Book Sales International Pty Ltd
76 Pymble Avenue, Pymble, NSW 2073
for
Golden Press Pty Ltd

First published 1986 by Golden Press Pty Ltd
Incorporated in NSW
5-01 Henry Lawson Business Centre, Birkenhead Point,
Drummoyne, NSW 2047, Australia and Auckland, New Zealand

ISBN 0 949220 00 0
©Book Sales International 1986

Designed by Martin Hendry
Typeset by David Graphic Sales, Sydney
Printed by Toppan Printing Co, Singapore

The picnickers came despite the name

Shark Bay, with its busy Nielsen Park Beach, has always been a favourite with Sydneysiders and visitors. In the '20s the ferry would drop bathers and picnickers off for a day's outing and the tea rooms did a thriving business. Dominating the area behind the beach is Greycliffe House (these views were taken from Greycliffe Avenue looking west). The mansion was built by William Charles Wentworth on his property of 100 acres (40 hectares) bought on June 4, 1827. His Vaucluse House is a Sydney landmark but the lesser-known Greycliffe House was built for his daughter, Mrs Reeve, in the late 1840s. On Wentworth's death the house passed to his son and was resumed by the government in 1913. This old view in mid-summer sees the *Kanangra,* built in 1912, just off the bay. *Kanangra* and her sister ship, *Kirawa,* were the first of only a few steel-hulled passenger boats on the harbour. She was 149ft long and could carry 945 passengers. Today's view, on a fine day in late autumn shows the bay and the beach in one of its rare near-deserted moments, with the shark net untested.

The days before Shell Oil

One of the first photographs of the John Fell Oil Refinery, shortly after it was built in 1925 and just before it was bought by Shell in 1927 after a fire which killed the founder's son. In the background is Rosehill racecourse. The refinery was built on a very swampy area that was part of a grant made to MacArthur to graze sheep at Rosehill. Shell employees can recall vast flocks of water fowl invading the area as recently as 30 years ago.

Contents

Introduction

The twenties to the eighties. Sixty years of enormous change in Sydney. The twenties were gracious days; the eighties are more raucous, more hurried, more strident. But the city is beautiful — whichever cloak it wears. Some Sydney people remember those early scenes; oldtimers who were thrilled to see the paddocks and playgrounds of their youth again. And just as excited to see the 1985 version in full colour, taken from the same vantage point. Perhaps more than anyone they will enjoy *Sydney — a Pictorial Contrast*. But the beauty of Sydney through the years will warm everyone. The journey began with John Ennemark, a German migrant who formed EB Studios in 1917 with Miss Hilda Bridges (the E and the B of EB). Together they recorded their own black and white panoramic record of Sydney from 1917 through to the mid-40s. From their first studio in George Street they moved to a very narrow three-storey building next to Wynyard Station in 1927. John was followed in the business by his niece, Anne, who died in 1984, aged 105. The lifelong work of EB Studios

If Father Therry had had his way, Taylors Point would today be part of a booming northern suburb called Josephtown. The controversial Catholic priest — he was at loggerheads with the Anglicans and the Government throughout his 34 years in Sydney — was given a grant of 1200 acres (480 hectares) by Governor Richard Bourke in 1833. Bourke had newly arrived and reinstated Therry after he had been fired as Catholic chaplain by Governor Darling. The land stretched from Whale Beach to Newport and included Taylors Point, Clareville and most of Careel Bay where Therry built a small wooden church. He called it St Josephs, expecting one day to see the township of Josephtown grow around it. But the idea was ahead of its time and the church was moved to Narrabeen in 1918. In the '20s land began to be sold at Taylors Point and Clareville, then neglected corners of Pittwater. Taylors Point, which offered waterfront properties for sale, is today virtually the domain of one sprawling mansion.

was 'rescued' by Phil Gray and Peter McGill, a Sydney publisher, who saw that the same scenes from the same vantage points in 1985 would create a unique study of the changes in the harbour city. The result is *Sydney — a Pictorial Contrast*.

Behind the landmark of the Opera House, little has changed in the 55 years separating these photographs. The plans for Government House were prepared in London in the 1830s by the architect to Queen Victoria, Edward Blore. Construction was left in the hands of the Colonial Architect, Mortimer Lewis. It replaced the original Government House on the eastern side of Sydney Cove; that land was needed desperately for the expanding city and waterfront. On November 2, 1832 Governor Bourke filed this report to England . . . 'the present Government House is a collection of rooms built at different times by successive Governors, and is in consequence not only extremely inconvenient and unsightly but in such a bad state of repair as to demand the immediate expenditure of a large sum of money to render it habitable and decent. His plea fell on sympathetic ears and the plans for today's building were drawn up within five years.

The heart of the city

Light filtered down to the footpaths; there were quiet corners and cars were so cumbersome you could skip across the road happily. It was a sleepier, warmer Sydney in the twenties. The Metropole down by the Quay was the centre of attention; the meeting place for town and country. Steamers and liners pulled up at the Quay and ferries ruled the harbour. Then came the Bridge, ending the vehicular ferries and opening up the North Shore. Twin skyscraper cities challenge each other across the water today. Downtown Sydney may have changed . . . but it's still superb.

An oasis in the heart of the city

Wynyard Square is one of the forgotten corners of Sydney history. Originally the Military Barracks and the Parade Ground occupied 15 acres (6 hectares) in the heart of the area. When they were moved to Paddington in the 1850s there was a big sale of Crown land. But one small space was left open to commemorate the Barracks; Wynyard Square named in honour of General Wynyard, the commanding officer at the time. In the 1880s and '90s business premises were built on the eastern side of the Square and further reconstruction to the Square area was made in the 1920s and early 1930s when the underground railway was extended to new stations named Town Hall and Wynyard. They were later connected to the Harbour Bridge and the city circle. Today it is a pleasantly shaded oasis in the heart of the city where office workers eat their lunch and pigeons pick up the crumbs as the buses pound down York Street to the west (right) and taxis pull up outside the Menzies Hotel to the east.

How the city has changed in 60 years. Nothing shows the difference in the city skyline better, perhaps, than the GPO tower. In the 1920s it dominated the skyline, looking over the business heart of the city; sneering down at the commercial companies. By 1985 it has been dwarfed. Qantas, the Hilton, American Express, the ANZ . . . the giants of the corporate world . . . have outstripped the old tower. At the bottom of the steel canyon the tower looks up forlornly, a forgotten landmark in Sydney, no longer on the tourist's itinerary. And yet it is a gracious building. Work on the GPO began in 1874 and took six years to complete. The clock tower was tall and striking — literally, its peal of bells was a highlight in Sydney at the time. The tower was taken down in 1942; it was feared Japanese bombers would use it as a target. The government was reluctant to restore the tower and the clock after the war, claiming the costs didn't justify it. But the public reaction was stronger than bureaucracy anticipated and, though it took 17 years, the tower was finally put back. Appropriately the chimes rang out again for the first time on Anzac Day, 1964.

The Quay was king in the 1920s, built on mud flats which were re-claimed in the 1840s. P&O holds the prime position (far left), with a third 'funnel' on one of the company's liners sticking up straight behind the backward-sloping front two. The mysterious extra funnel is the roof of the fake medieval tram depot built in 1902, replacing Fort Macquarie. In turn it was pulled down in 1959, to make way for the Opera House. The ferry *Kulgoa* (Aboriginal for 'returning') steams back towards Circular Quay where the old Metropole Hotel stands proud, then the recognised meeting point for city and country visitors. On the right the *Marella* is moored at the Singapore Lines Dock. The 7,475 ton ship was a veteran of the Australian-Singapore service. Built in 1914 for the Kaiser she became an Australian vessel after World War I and was sold in November, 1948 to a South American Company, re-named the *Captain Marcos* and placed under the Panamanian flag. To-day The Opera House dominates Bennelong Point, skyscrapers with international names rule the city and it is the *Narrabeen* which is heading for the Quay. Tied up at the far right is the beautiful *Eye of the Wind,* an iron, square-rigged brigantine built in Germany (like the *Marella*) in 1911. She was an ocean sailing vessel with no engine and carried general cargo to the River Plate in Argentina, returning via England with hides. After World War I she was sold to Swedish interests and the Sydney company Adventure Under Sail bought her in Sweden in 1973. She was refitted and restored for two years before being re-launched into a career as a charter vessel.

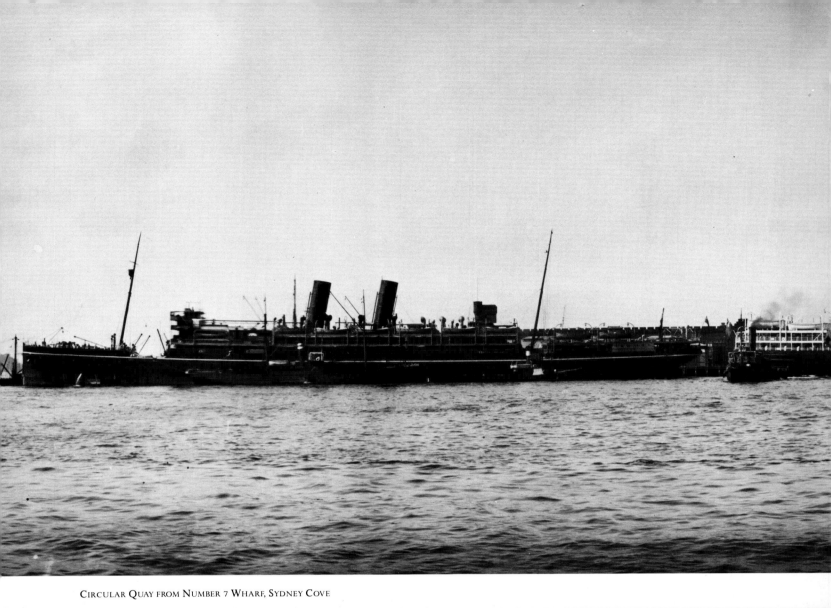

CIRCULAR QUAY FROM NUMBER 7 WHARF, SYDNEY COVE

THE CITY FROM THE ROOF OF THE NATIONAL BANK BUILDING, CORNER OF GEORGE AND BARRACK STREETS

Sydney & Harbour
from Church Hill

CHURCH HILL LOOKING NORTH — VIEW FROM THE ROOF OF A BUILDING IN YORK STREET

In this staggering demonstration of how much the city of Sydney has changed, one constant reminder of our past is St Philip's church, Sydney's first church. Begun in 1848 it reflects the West Country and Yorkshire origins of its architect, Edmund Blacket, with its strong but elegant tower. The clerestory windows above the main arches of the nave bathe the church in a soft warm light. In recent years St Philip's has been restored carefully and a modern parish house, in keeping with the changing city, was built in 1972.

The underground is underway

What a difference 60 years makes. Between 1924-26, when EB's photograph was taken, the underground railway network was being developed. Museum Station is boarded off (far left) and the carts and horses are probably carrying bags of sand excavated from Town Hall Station. The eastern tracks, passing through Museum and St James, were opened in December 1926. They virtually signalled the decline of the electric trams which had brightened the city streets since they replaced the steam trams in 1899. (The pedestrian 'safety zones' — those striped poles — form a barrier of sorts for tram passengers on Elizabeth Street.) The last Sydney tram, No 1995, ran on the afternoon of February 25, 1961 from Elizabeth Street to the eastern suburbs. More than 200 people squeezed on board for this historic journey, armed with screwdrivers and chisels to prise off a souvenir. In the end they virtually took the inside of the tram to pieces. Today the two giant slabs of Hyde Park Tower, which houses the NSW Electricity Commission, and Aetna Insurance's monument dominate the area.

The city on the harbour

The houses are expensive, the land is even dearer and the water views are almost priceless. Sydney is geared to living on the Harbour; to revelling in the panorama. And the Harbour has seen many changes...from the First Fleet to the growing cargo trade; from the prison ships anchored in mid-harbour to warships and spectacular ocean liners. The ferries, the first crude 18-footers, the luxury yachts and the hydrofoils. Houses, apartment blocks and parkland share the waterfrontage. And to cap it all, the Opera House . . . the Harbour's dress-circle arts centre.

SYDNEY HARBOUR BRIDGE, SYDNEY, 4:4:1930.

SYDNEY HARBOUR BRIDGE, SYDNEY, 1:11:30.

The Bridge of size

By April, 1930 the Bridge is beginning to take shape. The bottom sections of the two stone pylons already look majestic; stone masons were brought out from Scotland to provide the facing for the pylons from the Moruya granite quarry. Under the left-hand arch a vehicular ferry crosses the harbour. Their route from Dawes Point to either McMahons Point or Milsons Point came to a halt after the bridge opened two years later. The November 1930 view (bottom photograph) from McMahons Point has the span complete — the link was in August — and the suspension deck is being 'laid' as the creeper cranes return down the arches. The Bridge is, with Ayers Rock, Australia's best known landmark. The main span is 503 metres long and the combined length of the main span and the steel approach spans is 1149 metres. The arch is 134 metres above the mean sea level and made of silicon steel. The original central roadway was 17.4 metres wide but two lanes were added on the eastern side in 1959 by converting the former tram tracks. There are now eight motor lanes, railway tracks on the western side, a footpath on the eastern side and a bicycle path on the western side. The work was carried out under the supervision of Dorman Long and Company Ltd. Their workshops at Milsons Point were demolished after the bridge was completed in 1932 and Luna Park (opened 1935) sprang up on the site, despite cries from local residents for a foreshore park. Twelve men died while working on the Bridge itself and four others in associated work between the time the first spade was dug into the ground on July 28, 1923 and the controversial opening on March, 19 1932. The opening ceremony by State Premier Jack Lang was disrupted by Francis Edward de Groot, a member of the New Guard. Disguised as a military horseman he slashed the ribbon before the Premier. Ironically, this political demonstration captured more headlines for the Bridge itself than the original more mundane ceremony would have done. The cost of the Bridge has long been controversial...the state of NSW still services the original loan. But the actual New South Wales outlay appears to have been only eleven dollars! More than $3.3 million came from a levy imposed on northside property holders and $15.7 million was raised by loans. A further $21,000 came from unemployment relief funds which may or may not have been State money. The acting president of the North Sydney chamber of commerce, Jim White, claimed in 1985, that almost half the toll money collected each year was used to pay the salaries of the tollkeepers and described the toll in a letter to *The Sydney Morning Herald* as 'the most discriminatory and wasteful in Australia's history'.

THE HARBOUR BRIDGE TAKING SHAPE — VIEWS FROM BENNELONG POINT (ABOVE) AND McMAHONS POINT (BELOW)

Eye-liners!

The 1932 view from the city side of the bridge was taken shortly before the opening on March 19. The *Strathnaver* is being eased round into Circular Quay by a Waratah tug watched by a handful of people standing on the bridge near the southern pylon as the ferries turn into the Quay from the Lane Cove and Balmain runs. The 22,283-ton *Strathnaver* was added to the P&O line in 1931, the dream of the P&O chief, Lord Inchcape. In spite of the Depression he pressed on with the 'Strath' ships. *Strathnaver* and her sister ship, *Strathaird* (22,568 tons) were both oil-fired with turbo-electric propulsion. They were the 'latest thing' in liners and an instant success. The span grows closer in 1930 and in the foreground the *Kookaburra* sits quietly. Built in 1907, the 180-ton ferry was 140 ft long and could carry 794 passengers. She was broken up in 1950. In today's view, the *Oriana* looks magnificent at the Overseas Terminal while on the right the *Captain Cook* cruise boat leaves Circular Quay on another harbour sightseeing trip.

THE HARBOUR BRIDGE AND THE LINERS STRATHNAVER (ABOVE) AND ORIANA (BELOW) VIEWED FROM BENNELONG POINT

SYDNEY HARBOUR FROM THE ROOF OF THE ASTOR APARTMENTS IN MACQUARIE STREET

The navy's pride of the harbour

A pre-war view of Sydney Harbour from the Astor Flats in Macquarie Street. Luna Park (opened in 1935) grins back from under the Bridge as the ferries pull out from Circular Quay past a visiting warship. Around Bennelong Point the smoke of the Manly ferry streams behind as she heads for mid-harbour and the two 10,000-ton, 8-inch cruisers *Australia* (nearer) and the *Canberra*. (The *Canberra* was lost off the Solomon Islands in August, 1942 in the Battle of Savo Island with the loss of 78 lives). The foreshore of Neutral Bay is still relatively uncluttered and the many blocks of flats have not yet dominated the suburb. Today's view from the same apartment block bears little resemblance. The Cahill Expressway winds past the Conservatorium of Music and heads behind the city skyscrapers which all but block the Bridge and obscure Luna Park. The Neutral Bay foreshore view is interrupted by the Opera House and in 1985, it's the Manly hydrofoil which skips across the harbour, heading to Fort Denison on its inward run.

Taking a punt on the peninsula

In the early 1920s, as the view from Battle Boulevarde, Seaforth, shows, a punt still carried cars, horse-drawn vehicles and passengers from the Spit Terminus across to Middle Harbour. The first regular crossing was made in 1850 with a hand punt run by Peter Ellery. He charged passengers sixpence a crossing and horse traps one and sixpence. The steam punt was introduced in 1889 when the government took over the service. In November, 1900 the electric tram service was extended from Mosman to the Spit and pressure mounted on the slow, old-fashioned service as traffic soared. In 1924 the premier Sir George Fuller, opened the first Spit Bridge. It was a 'temporary' structure which lasted until 1959! Today's steel and concrete bridge, costing $2.2 million when it was built, lifts ponderously to allow through the tall-masted sailing yachts moored at the lavish and busy marina.

Long Nose Point (centre) in 1919 — Mort and Simmons Shipyard on the eastern side — a dilapidated looking area — was where the ferry *Kulgoa* was built. Around the point, on the western side, stands a paddock with a tiny white sign barely visible on the foreshore. A retired ferry captain remembers it clearly. 'It was a hoarding promoting a dye called Tintex,' he recalled. 'And it read: "Never say dye, say Tintex".' The magnificent old home on the tip of Long Nose Point is still there in the modern photograph, though heavily disguised by the waterfront trees which have grown. Behind it a block of flats has sprung up also.

VIEW FROM MANNS POINT, GREENWICH, OF LONG NOSE POINT, BIRCHGROVE

RUSHCUTTERS BAY AND ELIZABETH BAY FROM THE CORNER OF YARRANABBE ROAD AND THORNTON STREET, DARLING POINT

Richness on the rim of the city

The changes in the city itself are highlighted superbly in these two views nearly 70 years apart. Centrepoint and the city skyline bear almost no resemblance to the view just after World War I. The million dollar homes of Elizabeth Bay (centre) and Darling Point (where these views were photographed from) are a long way in the future. The Cruising Yacht Club, with its handsome marina, is also a project of the future and only a handful of yachts sat at anchor in Rushcutter's Bay in 1918. The baths on the eastern side of the bay (foreground) were demolished in the 1970s. The arms which shelter Rushcutters Bay were each named after the wives of State Governors; Elizabeth Bay (to the west) draws its name from Elizabeth Macquarie and Darling Point was originally Mrs Darling's Point, in honour of Governor Darling's wife. Rushcutters Bay has its moment of glory each Boxing Day when the fleet sets sail for the Sydney-Hobart ocean racing classic.

ROSE BAY FROM WUNULLA ROAD, POINT PIPER

The highlight of the harbour

In mid-harbour, tucked behind a dark New Zealand-built schooner, is one of Sydney Harbour's longtime 'monuments'...the *Tingira*. Originally the *Sobraon* (2131 tons) she was built at Aberdeen in 1866 and made several voyages to Australia before stopping at anchor in 1891 to become a reformatory ship for delinquent boys. There she lay at her moorings for 20 years until, in 1911, she was taken over by the Federal Government and used to train boys who had signed up for the Royal Australian Navy. She was broken up in 1940. To her right, past the houseboats then allowed to sit in Rose Bay, is a vast sandy hill where, today, multi-millionaire Alan Bond has made his home. The old jetty has long been replaced and now marks the home of the Royal Motor Yacht Club.

E.B Studios
278 George St
SYDNEY

LB LAVENDAR BAY

A million-dollar bath house

The western side of Lavender Bay, opposite the site of Luna Park, in the early 20s when the big ferries still stopped at McMahons Point and the municipal baths (right) were a feature of the area. Land on the foreshore was first dedicated for baths and public recreation as early as 1868. In 1881 Cavill's Baths were opened and in 1905 these were replaced by two floating baths. The Lavender Bay Bath House was demolished in 1975. The bay was virtually deserted in the 1920s as a mooring haven but today a mixture of yachts are crammed together in the lee of Luna Park. Sails Restaurant stands alongside the McMahons Point wharf where a small private ferry service and the little ferries of the government service run a much reduced service. Blues Point Tower (left) dominates the end of the point.

MOSMAN BAY FROM NEXT TO THE MOSMAN BAY SAILING CLUB

Almost 100 years after Archibald Mosman established his large and smelly whaling station, Mosman Bay had become a palatial suburb, highlighted by Monterey, the grand three-storey brick and stone Federation mansion (rising above the trees on the foreshore left). Built at the turn of the century for a local surgeon, Monterey was almost derelict in 1972 when it was bought by Mr Bill Baker and transformed into a restaurant, convention centre and private hotel. A two-year interim conservation order was placed on Monterey by the Heritage Council on December 14, 1982 and it is now the centre of a battle between Mr Baker and the local council. He claims it would cost more than half a million dollars to carry out fire safety work required by the council. Below Monterey in the 1920s scene are the metal hoppers owned by the council. Small steamers came from Kiama to drop their metal chips into the hoppers. Local residents complained about the noise and they were moved to the Spit. To the right of the hoppers is the old Mosman wharf, demolished in the 60s and further round the Bay, the boatshed of H.N. Colley and the private ferry company of Charles Rosman (the second half of the sign has fallen down). Started in 1906 the company is still run by Charles Rosman's son, who is now 85.

A city on the ocean

The early settlers gamely pounded their way to the beaches of Manly and Bondi for a chance to flop in the surf. Gradually the beaches more distant from the city found a following . . . Newport and Cronulla; Avalon and Palm Beach. Manly . . . Seven miles from Sydney and a thousand miles from care . . . was still the main attraction in those carefree years of the twenties. And from Manly, as cars became more popular, the Peninsula developed. Bondi, then and now, symbolises Sydney's ocean lifestyle. Even in winter the hardy and the joggers share the sand . . .

CRONULLA BEACH FROM OZONE STREET

The loo with a view

Cronulla in the early 20s, an uncrowded beach for the southern residents. The lifesaver in front of his reel watched the bathers in the shallows. The ladies dressing rooms had a prime beachfront position; the gentlemen were further back in the centre. On the hillside surveying the beach, the then Munro Flats (right), built in 1918 and becoming the Cecil Hotel in 1926. Today the Cronulla Sports Complex at Number 1 The Esplanade, has the magnificent site to the right of where the ladies dressing rooms stood, while behind it the Cronulla RSL commands a superb view of the beach. The palm trees immediately behind the beach have sprung up where once there was just windswept bushes and rough grass.

Looking south over Newport Beach from above Barrenjoey Road

EB Studios
Photo
278 George St
Sydney

Cars ran right on to Newport Beach in the 1920s. Picnicking was a leisurely, less hectic affair — certainly there were no parking fees! Newport was still a scattered, relatively remote area. The first settlers had arrived there in the early 1800s. Cattle and horses grazed contentedly in the paddocks while day trippers gazed in awe at Bungan Castle on Bungan Head, the dream of art dealer and agent Adolph W. Albers who first saw the headland on a sulky ride in 1918. The following year he bought the land for $800 and built his castle for $2200. In the 1920s it became notorious for the wild artists' parties he threw. Today it is ringed by suburban 'castles' some hovering even nearer to the cliff edge than Mr Albers' dream. And the parking? It's a much more orderly, though less romantic, affair...on a neat macadamised strip back from the beach.

A pioneer conservationist

A near deserted Avalon Beach of the mid-1920s viewed from the walk-way to the rock baths at the southern end of the beach. The magnif-icent Norfolk Pines are mere saplings with picket safety fences around them. Estate agent Arthur J. Small had begun sub-dividing land in the area but the beach area was still untouched. Small was a pioneer con-servationist who insisted the natural flora of the district be retained as much as possible. Small, allegedly, dreamed up the name Avalon in the middle of the night. The name, in Celtic mythology, described a paradise island but it is just as likely he went to sleep humming, the tune of *Avalon,* the Al Jolson 'hit' of the time. Small would be pleased with the beach today. The pines have grown tall and new saplings are protected for the future. The only development on the beach is the Avalon Surf Club and the immediate area behind the sand is an official recreational reserve.

The first mansion of Palm Beach

Looking up Palm Beach, across the baths and from the southern end. Villa d'Este, built in 1920 and named after a celebrated Italian mansion, is seen to advantage among a handful of less expensive but still lavish 'weekenders'. The Barrenjoey Lighthouse stands forlorn on Barrenjoey Head. At this stage the light is still powered by kerosene and is a fixed red glow. It took 15 months for the light to be installed and two men died in the battle to establish a permanent warning device. When it was operational on August 1, 1881, the first lighthouse keeper was a George Mulhall who lived in a stone cottage near the foot of the 11 metre tower. He was killed by a bolt of lightning during a storm as he gathered firewood. In August 1932 the original light was replaced by an automatic white flashing beacon. Today, Palm Beach is a much more discreet and elegant area; the saltwater baths are certainly the best maintained and most inviting of all the Sydney rock pools.

LOOKING NORTH ALONG PALM BEACH FROM ABOVE THE ROCK POOL

BONDI BEACH FROM QUEEN ELIZABETH DRIVE

The Royal Command Surf Carnival at Bondi Beach on February 6, 1954. Canvas deck chairs line the sand as the clubs parade for Queen Elizabeth and the Duke of Edinburgh. More than 12,000 people crowded the beach esplanade for the event. The 64-man guard of honour was a feature of the day. Each member of the guard was from a different club and wore his club's costume and cap. The Royal Couple seemed enthralled with the display and over-ran their original timetable by 40 minutes. The 1985 scene, taken on a sunny winter's morning for contrast, shows the sweep of the beach with the development along the northern front. A handful of swimmers are braving the cold water with the odd jogger and stroller enjoying the thin sun.

Pining for the past

In the late '20s Manly was thriving . . . so too were its famous Norfolk Pines, first planted along the esplanade in the 1870s. Today they are struggling to survive the twin threats of whipping sea spray and car exhaust pollution. The Manly Baths (foreground) have already lost the unequal struggle. They were pounded by violent storms in the 70s and were finally dismantled in April 1976.

MANLY BEACH FROM THE STEPS AT THE SOUTHERN END

A city and its suburbs

A handful of wooden shops and a dirt road intersection. The Caringbah of 60 years ago bears no resemblance to the thriving southern suburb of today. Or the major intersection at Mona Vale where Palm Beach and Church Point traffic part company: sixty years ago the same turnoff was a dirt corner where the market gardeners began their long trek to the Spit punt and Sydney. The Northbridge of today was a crude development road with scrub-covered hillocks; even Marrickville had open land ready for sub-division.

Subdivision comes to Northbridge in the early '20s. The power poles are in, roads are being carved from the bushland, a suburban boom is about to be launched. In the distance Beauty Point, Cremorne, Spit Road and Military Road are already well settled. The North, however, is still relatively deserted... the Spit Bridge has not yet been built and a steam punt carries travellers across Middle Harbour. What a contrast today. Trees planted by the new 'settlers' dominate the suburb with its cosy red roofs. The Spit has been all but obscured although the money-rich marina shows how successful the area has become.

The lamplighter's last stand . . .

It's 1919 — and the gas lamps still light the streets of Waverley near the Council Chambers in Bondi Road. As early as 1883 electric lighting had been proposed in the area but the first electric lights were not switched on until Febuary 1, 1922. And that marked the end of the old lamplighter who would make his rounds through the suburban streets turning on the gas lamps. In 1913 a portion of the northwest corner of Waverley Park was allotted as a site for the council chambers pictured and the council met for the first time in its new chambers on January 6, 1914. Part of the 1913 chambers still forms the shell of the present chambers although extensive alterations in the sixties and seventies have changed its appearance. The Water Reservoir on the hill — today almost totally hidden by the now mature vegetation — looks over the war memorial unveiled by the Governor-General Sir Ronald Crawford on December 15, 1918.

VIEW FROM THE KNOLL, BYORA CRESCENT, NORTHBRIDGE

VIEW FROM MONS AVENUE, MAROUBRA

The killer track

In early 1925 work went ahead at full throttle on the Maroubra Speedway. Opened on December 5, 1925 the Speedway had a short life, closing down only 18 months later. Some of the drivers who took on the steep embankments were to have an even shorter life...the speedway claimed a number of lives and earned the title of 'the Killer Track'. Seventy thousand people crowded into the grounds on opening night to see the racing cars of the day — Alvis, Jowett, Ballot and Bugatti. The cars tore round the steep banks at 100mph (160km/h). The track had been open less than a month when it claimed its first victim, Albert Vaughan, who rocketed straight over the wall in practice and was killed instantly. Sydney's champion, Phil Garlick, died the same way as did Freddie Barlow. Competitors began to desert the track and the crowds turned to the newly opened Speedway Royale. In 1934 the Light Car Club held a meeting at Maroubra in an attempt to revive the course but it was a failure. Today it is the Coral Sea Park, a large Housing Commission Estate.

LOOKING EAST FROM KANGAROO STREET, MANLY

In the '20s, St Patrick's College stood high on North Head, looking down benevolently over the beach which was 'seven miles from Sydney and a thousand miles from care'. Sixty acres (24 hectares) were given to the Catholic Church in 1879 by the government and in Novermber, 1885, the foundation stone for the college and episcopal residence was laid by Cardinal Patrick Moran. Today blocks of residential units dwarf the college. Reduced too are the fine Norfolk pines which once flourished on the seafront and in many of the back streets of Manly. The credit for the pine trees is controversial but the Father of Manly, as he was called — Henry Gilbert Smith — certainly saw that many Norfolk Pines were planted on the Esplanade as well as encouraging others to plant them in their own streets.

A fork in the old dirt road

Almost 70 years ago, today's major intersection at Mona Vale — where the road to Church Point branches off to the left and Palm Beach to the right — was a dirt patch criss-crossed by the tracks of the sulkies, traps and carts. A sign points to La Corniche, a restaurant and guesthouse named after the famous road connecting Nice and Mentone on the French Riviera. After the French owner gave it up, La Corniche became a guest house, a tea-rooms, an officers' training school during World War II and finally a country club venture which failed. Today it has been replaced by a block of home units. And the Tea Gardens (left) where the horses and carts pulled up is now a bottle shop and pizza parlour. Mona Vale, when this old scene was captured, was then primarily a farming community. Produce was taken laboriously to the city markets by horse and cart, crossing Middle Harbour on the Spit punt, pulling up Parriwi Road and finally having to cross the harbour at McMahons Point . . . a 12-hour journey.

The famous — or infamous — Sydney Stadium is going strong but to the right the old Chinese market garden land is still vacant. White City, opened November 21, 1921, home of the NSW Lawn Tennis Association and retaining the name of an old fun park formerly on the site, has not yet been built. (The NSW Tennis Association moved out of their Double Bay home in 1919 after running out of land.) In the foreground Victoria Place is today the All Nations Club. But it was Sydney Stadium, demolished to make way for the Eastern Suburbs Railway, which was notorious in the area. The legendary all-round sportsman Snowy Baker was synonymous with the Stadium. Promoter Hugh D. McIntosh snapped him up after the 1908 Olympics as a boxing referee for the newly-opened stadium. In 1911, Baker formed a syndicate and bought the stadium from McIntosh. This was shortly after one of his memorable nights at the arena...Baker was refereeing a bout between Australian Tim Land and American 'Cyclone' Johnny Thompson. Another American, middleweight Jimmy Clabby, leapt into the ring and accused Baker of being less than unbiased with his judgements. Baker measured him off and dropped him on the canvas with a classic left. End of discussion. But the most sensational of Baker's nights at the Stadium was on July 18, 1914. The Maitland and Australian idol Les Darcy, just 19, lost a points decision to the American ring veteran Fritz Holland. The Governor-General of the time, Sir Ronald Munro-Ferguson, had to be escorted to Baker's office as 16,000 Darcy fans erupted and broke every window in the Stadium.

Caringbah in 1920 . . . just a handful of wooden stores at the corner of the Kingsway and Port Hacking Road. The Kingsway was laid down by the Holt-Sutherland Estate Land Company Ltd in conjunction with the State Government. The steam trams ran between Sutherland and Cronulla from June 12, 1911 for nearly 20 years. From a depot near the present Sutherland Railway Station they went to Highfield (the original name for Caringbah) and then on to Curranulla Street (Cronulla Street) and the terminus. The run was not without incident. In November, 1924 the 6.37am from Cronulla lost control on the Miranda downgrade and overturned, killing the driver. The last passenger tram ran on August 3, 1931 and the last goods tram in December, 1932. They were replaced by buses which proved a disaster for the residents. The buses would not cater for the extra demand at weekends or on public holidays and the owners were quick to cancel an unprofitable run. But the trams had opened up Cronulla exactly as the trains had done for Sutherland some years earlier.

The corner of The Kingsway and Port Hacking Road, Caringbah

LOOKING OVER RUSHCUTTERS BAY FROM BAYSWATER ROAD, KINGS CROSS

VIEW FROM THE RAILWAY STATION ENTRANCE, ILLAWARRA ROAD, MARRICKVILLE

The Riverdale Estate — 58 shops and home sites — to be auctioned on August 14, 1920, had a grisly past. It was near here that one of the grand figures of the area, Dr Thomas Wardell, was murdered. On September 7, 1834 he was shot by bushrangers on his own estate which covered a massive 600 hectares (1500 acres) including all of present day Dulwich Hill, Marrickville and a large part of Petersham. The body was discovered by his servants the next day near a creek which ran down near the site of Marrickville Railway Station. Two men were hanged after a third turned King's Evidence against them. Dr Wardell had built his fortune after coming to Australia in 1824 and setting up practice as a lawyer before founding *The Australian* newspaper. Marrickville, named after Marrick, a small village in Swaledale, Yorkshire, is today a battling inner-city suburb with nothing of the drama of its past life.

Two prime home sites . . .

Two magnificent home sites in Neutral Bay between 1922 and 1924. Today grand houses stand on Marshall and Dempster's blocks on the corner of Hayes and Mann Streets. Sixty-odd years ago the trams still ran up the steep hill from the Neutral Bay wharf. The tram service finally closed on May, 26, 1956.

A city at play

The jostle at the turnstiles and the queue for a racebook, Sydney is a punting city and Randwick is its heartland. The SCG where the cricketing establishment or the Rugby League stars of the twenties would be astounded today to see the VFL migrants, the Sydney Swans, playing Australian Rules. The crowds that choked Coogee to see the shark net unveiled, the bowling clubs and the speedways — Sydney lends itself to play. And in the shadows of the past a hint of the dances and picnics that were so popular at Clifton Gardens. A city where every worker can be a millionaire for a day.

Shark nets, piers and public celebration

November 16, 1929. A milestone for Coogee. The mayor, Alderman J.T. Jennings officially opened the shark proof net after a mile-long procession through the streets of Randwick and Coogee. Throughout the day more than 130,000 people were said to have turned up to see this 'modern marvel'. The year before, Coogee Pier had opened: the dream of the Coogee Advancement League which had visions of another 'Brighton Pier'. A private syndicate built the pier at a cost of 70,000 pounds. At night the sharkproof enclosure was floodlit and night surfing — 'a joy hitherto only dreamt of, was inaugurated for the first time in any part of the world'. But the pier failed to live up to its expectations and was demolished in 1934; the net, too, was dismantled after falling into disrepair during the war.

A large crowd of 42,000 turned up to the England-NSW Rugby League clash. These were the golden days of Sydney sport when there were few rival entertainments. England won 10-5 though the scoreboard at this stage has them in front only 7-5 and NSW in there with a chance. It takes a Test or a grand final to draw a crowd like that today. The VFL (Victorian Football League) hoped to take Sydney by storm when the transplanted Sydney Swans brought Australian Rules to Sydney for the first time in March, 1982. Prime Minister Bob Hawke, the club's Number One ticketholder was there to see them win their debut match against Melbourne 137 to 108. Sadly, their form never lived up to the start. In this 1985 match recorded on May 26, they slid to 10th place on the VFL ladder after losing to Geelong, 13.11. (89) to 16.21 (117) before a crowd of 12,577. The Swans, in red and white, were formerly South Melbourne and battling to stay alive in the Melbourne Australian Rules competition when they made the interstate switch. They had played in the premiership for 48 years without a title and had not appeared in a grand final for 36 years. They were losing money heavily and at the end of the 1981 season were reported to be more than $500,000 in the red.

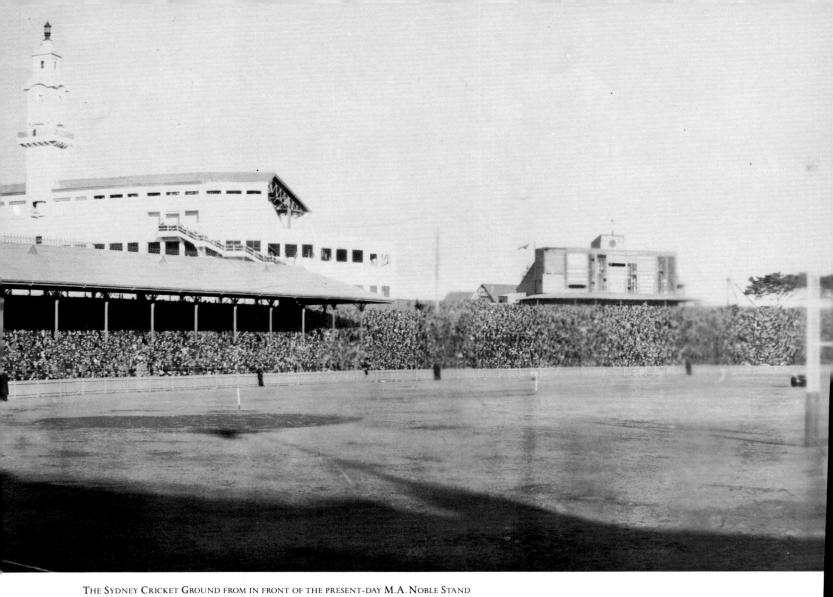

THE SYDNEY CRICKET GROUND FROM IN FRONT OF THE PRESENT-DAY M.A. NOBLE STAND

LOOKING NORTH FROM THE ROOF OF THE GRAND PACIFIC PRIVATE HOTEL, CORNER OF CARR AND BEACH STREETS, COOGEE

On the green at the Randwick Bowling Club

LEAGUE FOOTBALL MATCH.........ENGLAND v. N.S.WALES.
...June 7TH 1924...
WON BY ENGLAND.... 10 TO 5   ATTENDANCE 42,000.

A man and his trombone

Ray Richards is 79 now but he still turned up for a modern revival of an old tradition at the Randwick Bowling Club. Any members of the Randwick Municipal Band who were available would turn up at the club for the ceremonial rolling off the first bowl of the new season. (In the December 13, 1930 photograph, Mrs A.J. Bardon, wife of the club president is performing the honours). The Randwick Bowling and Recreation Club was formed on March 20, 1893 after a provisional committee of eight raised 120 pounds to lay the grass and a further 450 pounds for the clubhouse. Mr Richards joined the band in 1924 as a youngster of 18 and played at the club in the new season 'gala performance' that first year. Sadly, the happy tradition died out before World War II. In the 1930 view he is the trombonist on the left and in 1985 he is ninth from the left.

The crowd was reported unofficially to be a massive 300,000 that historic day in 1928 when Charles Kingsford-Smith — 'Smithy' — made the first crossing of the Pacific after battling violent storms between Suva and Brisbane. He landed in Brisbane on June 8 after a 21 and a half hour struggle to cover the 1900 miles in the *Southern Cross*. After a short stop he took off for Sydney and this amazing welcome. The American flag, the Stars and Stripes, signifying the takeoff on May 31 from San Francisco, flew along with the Australian flag as police surrounded the plane and kept photographers and the public at a safe distance. Today, Mascot, seen from the TAA Terminal, is a maze of runways — cramped and unable to cope with the flood of domestic and international flights.

Those picnics of the past

Chowder Bay, around 1925, was one of the North Shore's most popular picnic grounds with the hotel, dance hall and the giant saltwater circular baths of Clifton Gardens. The splendid three-storeyed hotel looked over the beach and the four-level diving tower attracted daredevils and experts from all over Sydney. The annual Butchers Picnic was a huge event at the beach, the holidaymakers streaming by the ferryload for dancing, picnicking, swimming and 'much merriment' according to a report of the time. Today, Clifton Gardens and Chowder Bay remains one of the great unspoilt corners of Sydney. All the resort facilities that made the bay so popular were taken down by the mid-60s. The old circular baths have been replaced by a long jetty, though there is still a sharkproof jetty bath. A recreational reserve behind the beach runs into a small Sydney Harbour National Park.

Game, set and match . . .

Sir Philip Woolcott Game, GBE, KCB and DSO, inaugurated as NSW Governor in 1930. Sir Philip, an Air Vice-Marshall, served from May 29, 1930 to January 15, 1935 and became the state's best-known governor. He had a mixed term; pre-empting the Sir John Kerr sacking of Gough Whitlam by 50 years. He used his powers on May 13, 1932 to dismiss the NSW Government of Jack Lang during a fearful battle between the State and Federal Governments. On his return to England in 1935 Sir Philip was appointed Commissioner of Police at Scotland Yard. But those years are ahead of him as he accepts the salute from the armed guard. The *Australia* stood off the jetty at the mouth of Farm Cove, her valuable 'cargo' having been delivered to Man o' War Steps by the *Lady Hopetoun,* the VIP launch. The Steps were built originally to give exclusive access from the water for visitors to Government House. Today the cranes of Garden Island have grown to rise above Mrs Macquarie's Point in the background. The Man o' War jetty is almost deserted while the carpark is dominated by an indicator board pointing to the various Opera House venues.

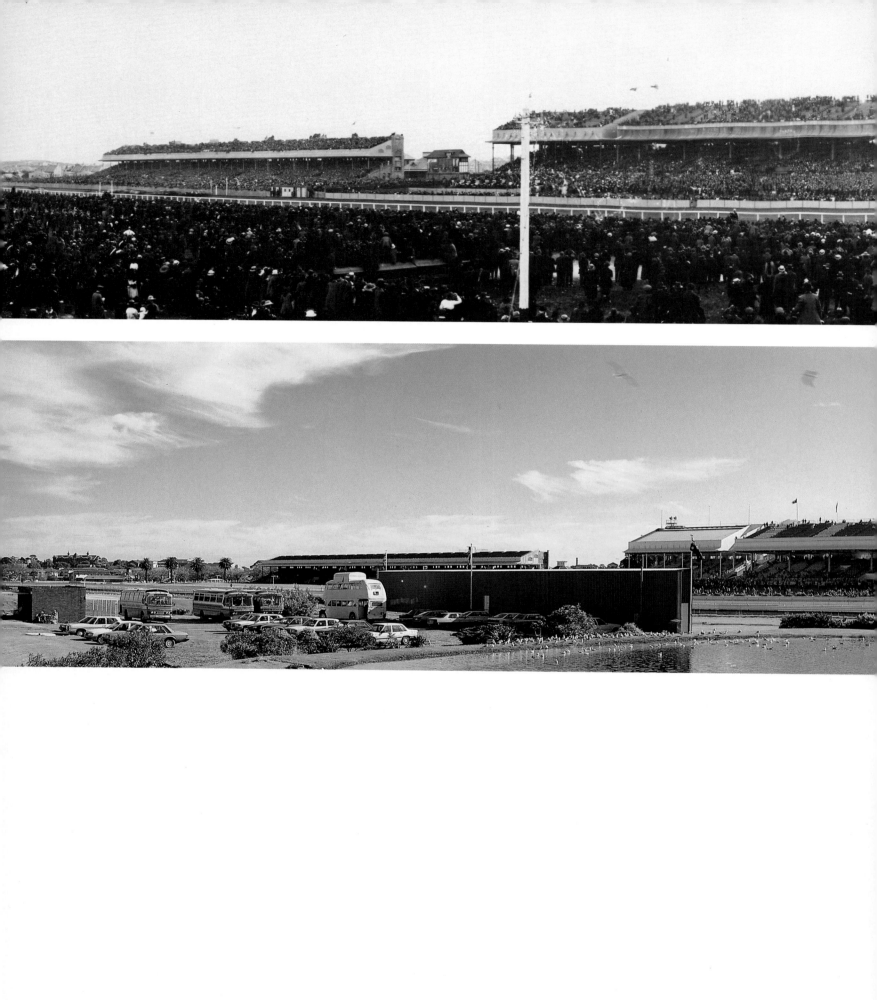

The sport of kings

A huge crowd turned up at Randwick Racecourse on Saturday, June 19, 1920 for the running of the Prince of Wales Gold Cup in honour of the visit of the Prince of Wales, later to become King Edward VIII. The feature event, the Prince of Wales Gold Cup, turned out to be a race fit for the sport of kings. Silverton and Parkdale fought out the last half-furlong locked together and they crossed the line in a dead-heat. Newcastle Cup winner Red Cardinal was third, only a head away. It was a right royal day for the bookmakers too — not one favourite won. *The Sydney Morning Herald* reported on the fashions of the day: 'Saturday's weather was ideal for the race meeting. The rain, which threatened early in the forenoon, rapidly cleared off and permitted the sun to shine out with almost spring-like warmth and geniality. Top coats, as a result — with the exception of a few elaborately trimmed with expensive fur or entirely composed of peltry — were discarded in favour of tailored suits, and the general effect was one of quiet colours, with relief given only occasionally by a bright-hued henna frock or hat decorations'. The second race on the 1985 Queens's birthday card was a much more mundane affair. Above the lake, Lethal, who led from the start, is coasting down the straight clear of Fix The Date and Perfect Jet.

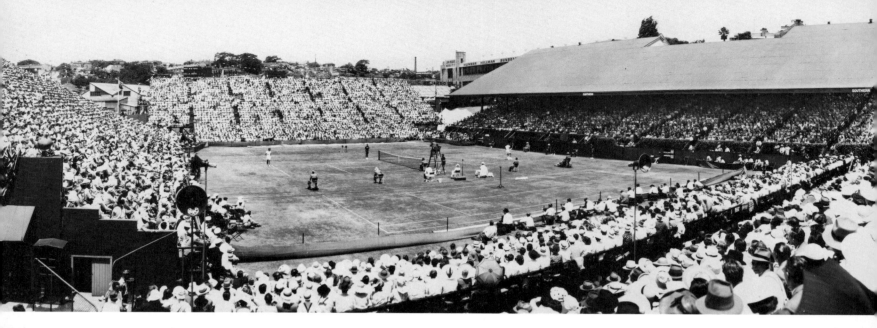

The days of polite tennis

It was a time of tantrum-free tennis. Those leisurely pre-television days when it was an occasion to dress for the Davis Cup, to clap politely and to cheer with restraint when your country won. And what a win it was in 1951, even if Australia got off to a poor start. A young Mervyn Rose, playing in his first Davis Cup singles match went down to Victor Seixas of the USA. It's one set each in this Boxing Day clash and Seixas went on to win 6-3,6-4,9-7 in 72 minutes. Frank Sedgman levelled the score when he beat Ted Schroeder 6-4, 6-3,4-6,6-4 and on the third day beat Seixas. Rose, sadly, went down to Schroeder in the singles but the doubles combination of Sedgman and Ken McGregor carried the day for Australia to retain the Cup by 3-2. What a contrast with the 1985 view of modern indoor tennis...the Johnson and Johnson Australian women's indoor championship at the Entertainment Centre, pink for the occasion. Boom microphones pick up every hissed annoyance and minor sound; plush seats and private boxes are laid on for the corporate customers. (Pam Shriver of the USA won the final on May 12, beating Australian Dianne Balestrat and picking up $75,000 prizemoney).

A city of little change

In 60 or 70 years, some corners of the city change very little. Vickery House at Waverley, 101 years old this year, or Government House. The stately grounds of Sydney University or the quiet oasis of Wynyard Square. In another 60-odd years they should be standing still. Gracious reminders of Sydney's past. Surprisingly some suburbs of Sydney look much the same as they did in the '20s; houses are brighter and the odd bit of renovation has changed a facade marginally but the past and the present are intertwined . . .

A healthy reminder . . .

The oldest faculty of medicine in Australia . . . the magnificent building of Sydney University photographed 54 years ago. The faculty formally began in June 1856 with the appointment of a board of eight medical examiners. But, although Sydney University 'got the jump' on Melbourne University by five years, it was the Melbourne institution which first awarded a medical degree. Today, the medical faculty is still one of Sydney's most gracious and beautiful buildings. Little has changed except the height of the trees.

Old 154 was a bargain

An old Brockway bus, unreliable and short-lived, trundles up Fullers
Road in 1933. The bus went from Chatswood Station to Fullers Road
via Lane Cove Road. The government ran the service for only one year
— it was uneconomical — and in 1934 sold poor old No 154 to a Mr
Pitman for just eleven pounds! The two houses still stand more than
50 years later but apart from the modern roads the area is surprisingly
unchanged.

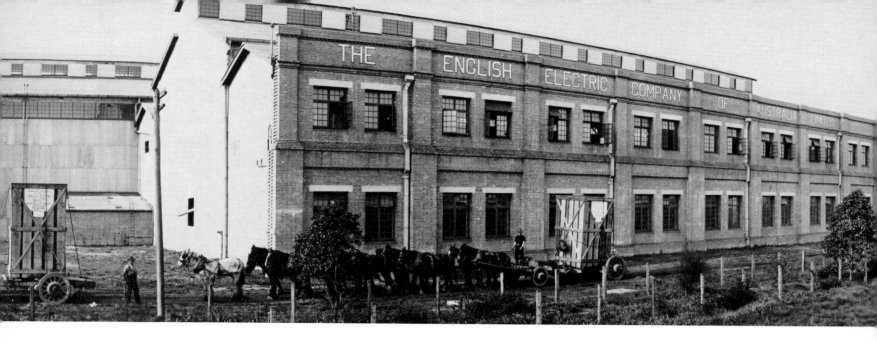

A 1921 view of the English Electric New Works, Berry Street, Clyde, when horses pulled equipment made for the Victorian Electricity Commission. Today it is the expanded home of the locomotive construction division of Comeng which, as Waddingtons, moved there in the mid-20s to produce custom-made bus bodies and railway carriages. Buses were manufactured on the site until the early '70s but the whole complex is now devoted to the design and manufacture of railway rolling stock.

The house the Vickerys built

Edina, the magnificent 101-year-old home on the highest ridge in the Eastern Suburbs, facing Birell Street and Carrington Street in Waverley, was built by Ebenezer Vickery, a leading leather and soft goods merchant. He was also the most influential Methodist layman in the State and the Castlereagh Street Methodist Centre was built mainly with his family money and named after him. The Vickery family lived at *Edina* until April 25, 1919 when the home was given to the church in memory of Ebenezer. At the same time the family was largely instrumental in establishing the War Memorial Hospital on the grounds. The National Trust describes *Edina* as 'basically five-bayed four square with a central front door and encased in an elaborately moulded, cement, two-storey verandah of arcaded Italianate design with projecting entrance porch and central tower accessible as a flat observation post'.

The photographer and his equipment

Phil Gray has always believed Sydney was the perfect city to highlight in the panoramic style. His discovery of the old EB negatives convinced him that this was the opportunity he had been waiting for . . . to create a modern study of Sydney drawing on the scenes of 60 to 70 years ago for contrast. But his problem was the modern camera equipment. Kodak had a magnificent old wooden Cirkut camera which faded away in the 1940s and nothing from Japan in recent times lived up to Phil's standards. He finally decided to have a camera built to his own specifications. A team of optical craftsmen in Europe created the $20,000 camera he used for this publication. Clockwork gears were replaced by three quartz-controlled mini-motors, the lens is the finest Schneider could offer and the camera has been constructed around the modern fine grain emulsions.

'That was the camera,' grins Phil. 'Then came the hard part — the shots themselves. Some of the scenes were almost impossible to relive 60 years later. Trees completely obscured the view or the original site had been so changed it couldn't be used. But gradually I found ways of reshooting the photographs that seemed to have historical importance.

'And I wanted to capture Sydney in all its moods, not just the hazy, brilliant days of summer that so many people seem to believe is the one picture of the city we should show to the world.'

But it wasn't just one man and his camera that made this book possible Phil stresses. 'I had so many people to thank when the shooting was over: 'My wife Nina who tolerated me being out of the house at all hours of the day and night in the hope of capturing the right moment and the right light. Without her support and help this book would have been next to impossible. My sons Philip and Simon, who helped proof and title the black and white panoramas.

'Jeremy Taylor, my assistant, kept the project running with caffeine and strudel interludes, Chris Hoskin, my secretary, kept us both on an even keel by co-ordinating the whole operation superbly and Noel Outerbridge for coping so efficiently in my absence.

'And of course the superb Kodak Ektachrome colour film, which complemented the hand-crafted camera and lenses. Finally, thanks to the lasting qualities of the Kodak black and white Cirkut film.'

PHIL GRAY AND HIS PANORAMA CAMERA

Index of locations

Acknowledgments

The publishers would like to especially acknowledge the help of the Royal Historical Society of Australia whose advisers and helpers unravelled so many fine points.

Also: George Smith (research); Pam Garland, Sutherland Shire Librarian; The NSW Rugby League; Rod Clarke (Adventure Under Sail); the Maritime Services Board; retired master mariner Ron Wayling; John Fairfax and Sons Library; Waverley Historical Society; Wellings Local History Collection (Manly Library); NSW Tennis Association; The Department of Motor Transport; Comeng Pty Ltd; Mosman Municipal Council; Stanton Library (North Sydney); Fisher Library; Randwick Municipal Council; Randwick Historical Society; Catherine Snowden, curator of the Historical Photograph collection at Sydney University; G.T. Hardwick; Ken Brownscombe; Ian Debenham, assistant curator, Museum of Applied Arts and Sciences; Peter Kogoy (The Sun newspaper); The Astor Pty Ltd; The Luna Park management; Sydney Church of England Grammar School, North Sydney; Board of Directors, War Memorial Hospital (Waverley); P. Benjamin (Whale Beach); Mr and Mrs W. Branch (Cronulla); Hartland and Hyde Pty Ltd; Shell Refining (Australia) Pty Ltd; Belinda and Frank Marshall (Rushcutters Bay); Willoughby Municipal Library; Irene and Victor Newman (Rose Bay); Mr and Mrs McConnell (Maroubra); SCG Trust; Sydney Swans administration; Leighton Contractors Pty Ltd; TAA; Arthur Mavros (Coogee); Johnson and Johnson Australia Pty Ltd; the members of the Randwick Bowling Club; Dr Donald Hipsley; Bill and Di Bracey (Parsley Bay); Frank Kirk (McMahons Point)

And very special thanks to Kevin Weldon, chief executive of the Weldon-Hardie Group, Betty and Colin Bullard of Melba Studios Pty Ltd and Barbara Perry and Sylvia Carr, National Library of Australia